Hide It in
Your Heart

When you lie down,
you will not be afraid;
When you lie down, your sleep will be sweet.
Proverbs 3:24

For the word of the Lord
is right and true;
He is faithful in all He does.
Psalm 33:4

Creative Ways for Families to Explore God's Word

GLORIA GAITHER & SHIRLEY DOBSON

Artwork by Carrie Hartman

Multnomah Gifts®
Multnomah® Publishers *Sisters, Oregon*

HIDE IT IN YOUR HEART

© 2005 by Gloria Gaither and James Dobson, Inc.
published by Multnomah Gifts®,
a division of Multnomah® Publishers, Inc.
P.O. Box 1720, Sisters, Oregon 97759

Artwork © 2005 by Carrie Hartman
www.carriehartman.com

International Standard Book Number: 1-59052-509-4

Design by Koechel Peterson, & Assoc., Inc., Minneapolis, Minnesota

Unless otherwise indicated, Scripture quotations are taken from:
The Holy Bible, New International Version ©1973, 1984 by International Bible Society, used by permission of Zondervan Publishing House

Other Scripture quotations are from: *The Living Bible* (TLB) © 1971. Used by permission of Tyndale House Publishers, Inc. All rights reserved. *Holy Bible*, New Living Translation (NLT) © 1996. Used by permission of Tyndale House Publishers, Inc. All rights reserved. *The Holy Bible*, English Standard Version (ESV) © 2001 by Crossway Bibles, a division of Good News Publishers. Used by permission. All rights reserved. *The Holy Bible*, New King James Version (NKJV) ©1984 by Thomas Nelson, Inc. *New American Standard Bible* (NASB) ©1960, 1977 by the Lockman Foundation. *The Holy Bible*, King James Version (KJV).

Multnomah Publishers, Inc., has made every effort to provide proper and accurate source attribution for all selections used in this book. Should any attribution be found to be incorrect, the publisher welcomes written documentation supporting correction for subsequent printings. We gratefully acknowledge the cooperation of other publishers and individuals who have granted permission for use of their material.

Multnomah is a trademark of Multnomah Publishers, Inc., and is registered in the U.S. Patent and Trademark Office. The colophon is a trademark of Multnomah Publishers, Inc.

Printed in Italy

For Information:
MULTNOMAH PUBLISHERS, INC. • P.O. BOX 1720 • SISTERS, OR 97759

05 06 07 08 09 10 11—10 9 8 7 6 5 4 3 2 1 0

To my parents, Lee and Dorothy Sickal, who loved
the Scriptures and loved me so much that they surrounded
me not with cold rules but joyful principles for real life—
the living, breathing, walking-around Word.
They not only told the Story; they *became* the story.

⁓

GLORIA GAITHER

This book is dedicated
to children around the world
who need, above all else,
to have a personal relationship
with Jesus Christ
and an intimate knowledge
of the Word of God.

⁓

SHIRLEY DOBSON

Table of Contents

God's Word Endures Forever

I was bounding through our old Michigan farmhouse on my way out to the orchard to eat snow apples and feel the summer breeze in my hair when I caught a glimpse of my daddy. He was sitting in the corner of the living room where he often sat, by the window. I made an abrupt turn to run to him before going outside. He wasn't "studying" at the table where he usually prepared his sermons but just sitting in his big, green, overstuffed chair. Over his right hand was draped this big "soggy" Bible, the kind of Bible preachers have, the kind I always wanted because it fell open and hung down limp on each side when held in one hand. Now my little eyes focused on Daddy's face. Tears were streaming down his tanned cheeks, but he wasn't sad. He scooped me up in his other arm and lifted me onto his lap, still holding the Scriptures in his right hand. I didn't need to ask. I knew why Daddy was weeping. Often I had seen him deeply moved by some beautiful or awesome revelation from the Holy Spirit while he was reading God's Word. These insights and illuminations were often the topics of our discussions at the supper table and the texts read for our nightly family worship time.

What has remained with me over the years of that memory was that my father wasn't reading the Bible to prepare a sermon or a Sunday school lesson. He wasn't reading to be a "good example" to me. I had just happened in on him spending time with Jesus and listening to God speak through His Word. God had spoken and I had entered a sanctuary; in my father's embrace I, too, sensed that we were on holy ground.

My parents made the Word a very practical part of our daily lives. In fact, it is impossible for me to think of life in tidy compartments labeled "sacred" or "secular," for all of life was sacred and the Scripture was very relevant to our "secular" Monday through Friday life.

I don't remember ever being required to memorize Scripture except during Vacation Bible School, held for two weeks every July at the little community church where my parents pastored. But somehow, by the time I left for college, huge portions of Scripture had been entered in my memory bank and had become a part of every fiber of my being.

When I became an adult and a young parent, I found myself wondering exactly *how* I had come to know and love the Scripture and *when* I was taught its meaning. I realized that my parents had taken seriously God's instructions to families from the ancient writings of Deuteronomy. Without my really noticing, they had made Scripture a part of our lives because it was a way of life for them. They had first of all taken God's Word into their own hearts, making it not something they *read* or even something they *did*, but something they *were*. And because the Word was in their hearts, they had "talked about it" while walking, sleeping, waking, and sitting—in the house, in the church, by the way, and at the table.

Every passage of our lives bore the stamp of God's Word: birthings, dying, marrying, comings of age, departings, returnings, and remainings all were solemnized with appropriate blessings and instructions from God's Word. In season, out of season, when it was convenient, when it was difficult, when we were sufficient, inefficient, self-sufficient, or insufficient, we read the Bible together, or someone was sure to quote it.

The truth and certainty of the Bible has been for me a plumb line, a measuring stick, and a compass in a crumbling culture where there are no moral absolutes. I have come to believe that equipping our families with the truth of the living Word is not an option, an opinion, or a persuasion. It is a life-and-death necessity if our children—and we ourselves, as their mentors—are to survive the disintegration of all we hold dear as the very foundations of society turn to powder under our feet.

Morality, integrity, industry, compassion, commitment, self-discipline, hope, tranquility, honesty, faithfulness, and dependability have never been instilled in human beings by the broad culture or strong public opinion or governmental policy. These enduring qualities are a result of parents and other significant adults teaching truths to children, verbally and by example. When children become mature enough—if the groundwork has been laid at home—they will realize these qualities are impossible aspirations without the empowerment of a transcendent God who alone can implement our highest human ideals.

Through the ages the Bible has been cherished and condemned. It has engendered devotion and denunciation. It has been ridiculed, banned, and burned. It has been dismissed and ignored. It has been embraced and treasured. Some have gone to their graves cursing and trying to abolish it; many more have died defending it. Scholars have been martyred for translating it for the common person to read. Kings have tried to make it the exclusive property of the aristocracy.

Voltaire proclaimed two and a quarter centuries ago that there would "not be a Bible on the earth except one that was looked upon by an antiquarian curiosity seeker." British bishops once called it "that damnable book." Tyndale had to flee to

Germany to translate it into English, only to see the six thousand copies that were smuggled back into England seized and burned. Tyndale was eventually captured and strangled, then burned at the stake. Cromwell ordered a copy of the English Bible made available in every English church, yet under Queen Mary I, printing of the Bible was punishable by death. Queen Elizabeth called it "the jewel I love best," yet she persecuted Roman Catholic scholars who then fled to the Continent and there translated the Rheims-Douay version.

But in spite of everything, the Bible has endured. Translations and paraphrases have made God's Word accessible to more men, women, and children than ever before in history. Despite Voltaire's grim prediction, more new copies are printed, sold, and read every year all over the world than ever before in history.

But the copies that are dearest to me are the ones I see nightly in my grown children's hands as they seek in its pages guidance for their young families and their own uncertain days.

As I finish this manuscript, I do not shake with fear, nor am I depressed by pessimism. I believe in the power of the Word of God, and I know that Isaiah's prophecy is true to the end of time: "The grass withers, the flower fades…but the word of our God stands forever" (Isaiah 40:7–8, NKJV).

A Parent's Most Important Task

Shortly after the collapse of communism in the former Soviet Union and the fall of the Berlin Wall, my husband received a visit from a Moscow sociologist named Mikhail Matskovsky. Dr. Matskovsky was responsible for family-related research and other scientific investigations in his country. He had come to the United States, and then to Focus on the Family, for a very specific purpose.

After a brief introduction and greeting Dr. Matskovsky said to my husband, "Let me tell you why I'm here. I want to talk to you about your belief system. I am an atheist, and I certainly do not understand your concept of Jesus Christ. We Russians must admit, however, that our 'god' died with the disintegration of communism. Now we are attempting to find a new way of thinking that will be good for our society. I have come to seek your help in identifying what might be called 'ultimate values.' Do you think the Ten Commandments would be a good place to start?"

My husband and the former Soviet official spent an hour talking about the truth of Scripture. It was interesting and encouraging to note that this social scientist recognized, even in the absence of a meaningful faith, that there was inspired wisdom to be found in the ancient Scriptures. I wish every American scientist and bureaucrat had the same appreciation for the Bible!

My own journey into the Word began when I was only eight years old. My mother sent my brother and me to a neighborhood evangelical church where I learned from a compassionate Sunday school teacher, Mrs. Baldwin, and from a Bible-teaching pastor, Reverend Penner, that God loved me and every member of the human family. Furthermore, I began to see in Scripture that God had told us how He wanted us to behave and why it was important to live by those principles.

With the encouragement of Mrs. Baldwin I memorized the Ten Commandments and began to see how they applied to my life. I understood that the Lord did not want me to lie or steal or be jealous of those who had more than we did. I saw the importance of putting God first in my life and letting Him guide my path. Ultimately, this understanding of Scripture led me to give my heart to Jesus Christ as my Lord and Savior. *That* was the pivotal moment in my entire life and has influenced everything occurring from that early experience to the present.

A few years later, this personal relationship with the Lord and the Scriptural principles I had learned held me securely as my family began to disintegrate. I had an anchor in the midst of the storm. It also held me steady during the turmoil of my adolescent years, when my friends and associates began to participate in immoral and destructive activities. I was exposed to the same temptations, of course, but ringing in my ears were those familiar Scripture verses I had stored away in my heart. For example I knew God was riding in the car with me when I was on a date, and I understood that He loved me. He wanted the best for me and had given His commandments to protect me from my own sinful desires. It was not fear of my mother's punishment or displeasure that kept me on the straight and narrow. It was respect for those biblical truths I had learned from Mrs. Baldwin and my pastor that made me want to do what was right. How unfortunate it is that many of today's children have no knowledge of what Dr. Matskovsky called "ultimate values."

A recent Gallup Poll revealed that only three percent of young people could name all ten of the commandments, and 15 percent could identify a mere one of them! As shocking as that revelation is, it should not surprise us. We have not bothered to teach these basic understandings of right and wrong to the next generation. In one of the most regrettable judicial decisions ever rendered, the United States Supreme Court ruled in 1980 that the state of Kentucky could not post the Ten Commandments on the walls of its schools. Even worse decisions were to come. In 1992 in the case of Casey vs. Planned Parenthood the court ruled that we as Americans are entitled to our own interpretation of reality. This was the first time we have as a people moved away from the idea given to us by the Founding Fathers that the Creator is the source of our rights and our values.

From that time to this, right and wrong have been determined not by God but by whatever the court says they are. Then there is the case of Lawrence vs. Texas. The court ruled that sodomy is protected by the constitution. May God have mercy on us!

Is it any wonder that so many teenagers today seem to be guided by no internal compass? Some can kill with no sense of remorse. Many become involved with sex and drugs while they're in middle school or even younger. Indeed, we appear to be approaching the period in human history Paul described in 2 Timothy 3:2–5:

> People will be lovers of themselves, lovers of money, boastful, proud, abusive, disobedient to their parents, ungrateful, unholy, without love, unforgiving, slanderous, without self-control, brutal, not lovers of the good, treacherous, rash, conceited, lovers of pleasure rather than lovers of God—having a form of godliness but denying its power. Have nothing to do with them. (NIV)

This depravity occurs when a culture begins to make up its own rules apart from God's moral law as occurred in ancient Israel when "each man did what seemed right in his own eyes" (Judges 21:25, KJV). Clearly, there should be a sense of urgency about the spiritual development of our children.

This description of a wicked and perverse generation is remarkably relevant to our day. The culture in which we live is threatening even the children from Christian families because of the pervasive influence of peer pressure. According to George Barna, only 9% of teens who profess a commitment to Christ say they believe in moral absolutes, and for teens who do not profess to be Christians, a scant 4% believe in moral absolutes. How can we guide our boys and girls through a social environment in which the only standard of right and wrong is public opinion? Rock stars and professional sports figures now have more influence on the behavior and beliefs of young people than do ministers or parents. To millions of teenagers physical attractiveness is far more significant than the content of one's character. As the professional tennis star, Andre Agassi, said in his television commercial, "Image is everything!" Agassi is wrong. Image is *not* everything. The immutable truths of God's Word must be the standard for our values and beliefs. Everything else is "wood, hay and stubble" (1 Corinthians 3:12–13, KJV).

To repeat the question many Christian parents are asking today, how can we shepherd our kids through the mine field of wickedness laid down by Hollywood and the secular media? There is only one secure answer: We must expose our children to the wisdom of Scripture from their earliest experiences. We cannot afford to be casual about that most important of assignments. Moses described the proper approach to this spiritual training when he wrote, "These commandments that I give you today are to be upon your hearts. Impress them on your children. Talk about them when you sit at home and when you walk along the road, when you lie down and when you get up. Tie them as symbols on your hands and bind them on your foreheads. Write them on the doorframes of your houses and on your gates" (Deuteronomy 6:6–9, NIV).

I wish every boy and girl today could come under the influence of a godly person like Mrs. Baldwin, who loved the Word more than her own life. Perhaps there is such a saint in the church to which you take your children. It would be unwise, however, to depend on someone else to handle this assignment. *You*, as a mother or father, are charged with the responsibility of training up your children in the way they should go.

That may be the most important task you will be given in your lifetime. No other accomplishments and no other success will compensate for failure to teach these eternal truths to the generation now around our knees.

My husband's grandmother used to gather her six children around her for daily devotions. Her prayer made such an impression on Jim's dad that he referred to it throughout his life. She prayed, "Lord, it is my most urgent request that each of these children will come to know You personally. If one of them fails to make that commitment, it would have been better that I had never been born." This is the priority she gave to her spiritual responsibility.

I encourage each of you to help your children hide the Word in their hearts. That is why we have written this book to assist in that critical task. It will be worth whatever inconvenience and effort is required to convey spiritual truths to your kids while they are young and pliable. As we know so well, nothing invested in a child is ever lost.

It is my prayer that the Lord will use the ideas we have provided here to help you instill "ultimate values" and eternal truths in the hearts and minds of your children.

GOD'S INSTRUCTIONS FOR LIFE

Since God created us, it stands to reason that He knows best what we need—and what we need to do—in order to experience maximum joy, health, peace, harmony, and glory for His kingdom. He also knows the things that might cause us to self-destruct. And He lets us know these things in the Bible. In fact, God's Word is like an operations manual for human beings. If we read the manual and do what it says, we will experience the best possible results for our lives as well as in our relationships with each other and with our Maker.

In this section you will find some of the instructions God has given us—and some fun ways to remember them and make them part of your life.

The precepts of the LORD are right,
giving joy to the heart.
The commands of the LORD are radiant,
giving light to the eyes.

Psalm 19:8

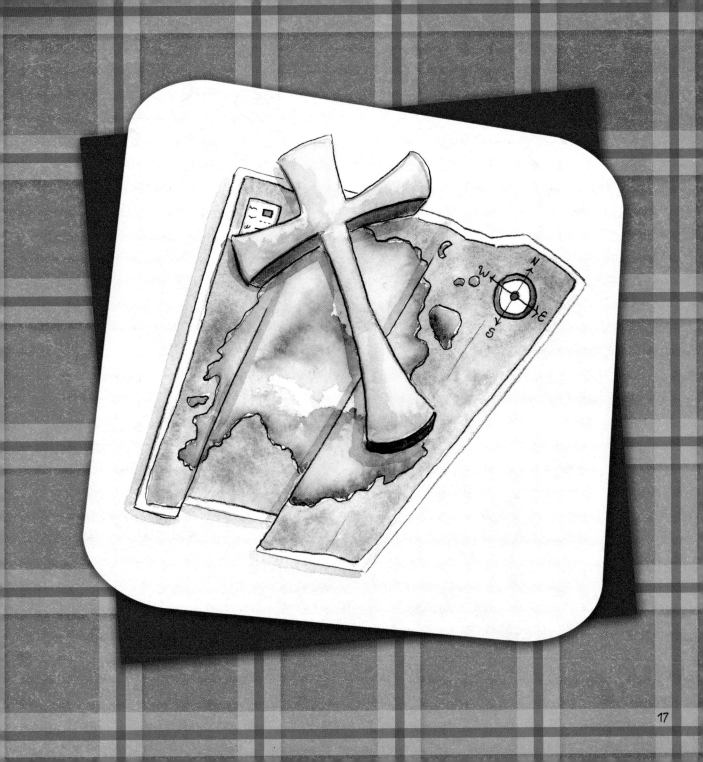

Communion in the Community

Most kids remember their five-year-old shots for a long time after they start kindergarten! Those not-very-fun immunizations are important for fighting disease.

Communities can get diseases too. Diseases like loneliness and fear, stealing and lying. But in the Bible God gives us immunizations against those diseases and others. They're the Ten Commandments. And, as someone once wisely observed, "The Ten Commandments are *not* the Ten Suggestions."

Imagine if everyone obeyed those commandments! People would be honest and trustworthy, dependable and fair. Well, we can get a taste of that kind of community at home when we love others the way we love ourselves. Yep, "Love God" and "Love one another" are Jesus' two-rule summary of God's Law! So let's start lovin'!

- Spend ten weeks studying the Ten Commandments together (Exodus 20:1–17). Each week focus on one commandment. Memorize it, talk about what it means, and figure out how each person in the family can obey that commandment in everyday life.

- Read the words of Jesus in John 15:12. In that second passage He tells us the cure for our tendency to break God's commandments: "Love one another." Give an illustration of the fact that thoughts and attitudes always come before our actions. For instance, what attitude precedes being mean to our little brother? What attitude comes before disobeying Mom? What thoughts precede the choice to copy someone's answers on a test?

- Okay, we already know that we break God's commandments. What can we do to "fix" our hearts and minds, to heal our thoughts and attitudes, so that our actions never hurt others or ourselves? What help can Jesus offer us as we try to do that fixing?

- What does Jesus say we must do immediately (before each day ends) when we fail to be loving and thoughtful? (See Matthew 5:23–24 and Ephesians 4:26.)

You shall not steal

You shall not take the Lord's name in vain

I am the Lord your God: You shall not have strange gods before me

Honor your father and mother

"'Love the Lord your God with all your heart
and with all your soul and with all your mind.'
This is the first and greatest commandment. And the second is like it:
'Love your neighbor as yourself.'"

Matthew 22:37–39

the Ten Commandments
Exodus 20:1–17

1 You shall have no other Gods before me.

2 You shall not make for yourself an idol in the form of anything in heaven above or on the earth beneath or in the waters below.

3 You shall not misuse the name of the LORD your God.

4 Remember the Sabbath day by keeping it holy.

5 Honor your father and your mother, so that you may live long in the land the LORD your God is giving you.

6 You shall not murder.

7 You shall not commit adultery.

8 You shall not steal.

9 You shall not give false testimony against your neighbor.

10 You shall not covet your neighbor's house.

What do you love? Pizza? Chocolate ice cream? Kittens? Your mom?

The Lord makes it clear what we should love more than anything—and actually that "what" is a "who." And that "who" is Him! We should love God more than we love anything or anyone! Read the first commandment in Exodus 20:3.

- When we love someone, we want to spend time with that person. We want to talk to and listen to that person. We don't want to disappoint, anger, or hurt that person. What do you do to show God that you love Him?
- Many people today love driving fancy cars, having lots of clothes, living in a big house, and owning cool toys. When we love those things, we're actually loving money, what people think of us, and ourselves. Why doesn't God want us loving these things?

The second commandment and the third commandment fit with the first commandment. Read Exodus 20:4 and 7.

- Why doesn't God want us to make idols?
- Why is obeying the second commandment also obedience to the first commandment?
- What does God command in the third commandment?
- Why is honoring God's name a way of loving Him?

Jesus helps us understand the first three commandments when He tells us which command is the most important one God has ever given. In Matthew 22:37 He teaches, "'Love the Lord your God with all your heart and with all your soul and with all your mind.' This is the first and greatest commandment." If you obey this command, you'll be obeying the first three—if not four!—of the Ten Commandments!

Keeping God's Day Holy

God's fourth commandment to His people was to keep one day each week holy—different, set apart, and distinct from the other six days. When Jesus came, He did not get rid of this commandment. Instead He taught that our observance of the Sabbath should affect the other days of the week by reminding us that all the time we are given, every moment of every day, is a sacred gift from God's hand and that we should live each day with gratitude to Him.

Because Jesus arose from the tomb on the first day of the week, most Christians celebrate Sunday as the special, holy, and set-apart day. Here are some ways your family can remember the Sabbath day to keep it holy.

- Go together to a place of worship and join with other believers in singing, worshiping, and learning about God.
- Try to avoid arguments, angry words, or bickering on God's special day.
- Eat together as a family—and invite others who are alone or away from home to join you.
- Don't work on this day. God said it was to be a day to rest our bodies, minds, and spirits.
- Refrain from shopping on this day. Even though many stores are open on Sunday, get your shopping done on another day so that the Lord's Day is not used for commerce.
- Honor God by agreeing not to play secular music on the Lord's Day. Use this day to listen to Christian recordings and to sing hymns and spiritual songs together for encouragement.
- Enjoy God's creation and take time to really notice the sky, the grass, the birds, the trees, and all the beauty we too easily rush past on other days. Go on a walk alone or with your family. Take deep breaths of the fresh air as you use the time to pray and give thanks to God.

- Rest. Take a nap and let sleep restore your body and mind.
- Read poetry and stories that are uplifting or a book about God's goodness in someone's life.
- Read God's Word aloud together and see what you can learn from a Bible story.
- Spend some time in a good conversation with relatives and friends, old and young. Don't hurry. If the weather is nice, sit for a spell on the front porch or in the garden.
- Focus on positive things and then be sure to thank God for them!

The "Promise" Commandment

Did you know that only one commandment comes with a promise? It is the fifth of God's Ten Commandments, and it reads like this:

> Honor your father and your mother,
> so that you may live long in the land
> the LORD your God is giving you.
>
> Exodus 20:12

Why do you think God promised that if we obey our parents, we will have a long life?

1. List some things you can learn (or have learned) from your parents that will keep you safe, or even save your life. (Parents, if you still have parents, discuss answers to this question as a family.)
2. Now list all the things God wants parents to teach their children and how each would give them a long, happy life "in the land"—and even into eternity. Come up with suggestions for how to teach these things.

Look up and read the following verses:

Psalms 37:25–26; Proverbs 22:6; Psalms 103:17; Matthew 11:25; Matthew 19:14.

God's Word is full of promises to enrich your life if you are a parent raising your children to know and love and serve the Lord or if you are living with your parents and want to do so God's way and receive His blessings.

All your children will be taught by the LORD, and great shall be the peace of your children.
Isaiah 54:13, ESV

honor your father and your mother • honor your father and your mother

Pure Gold!

Love your neighbor as yourself

Remember how our obedience to the first and "greatest" commandment will automatically be obedience to the first four of the Ten Commandments? Well, there's a shortcut to obeying the other six—but before we reveal the shortcut, let's take a good look at them first.

You already know that "Honor your father and your mother" is number 5. Now read Commandments 6, 7, 8, 9, and 10 in Exodus 20:13–17.

- You might think Commandment 6 will be easy to obey, but Jesus teaches that we take life out of our relationships with our words. Think of a time when someone's words hurt you. Think of a time when your words hurt someone else, maybe your brother or sister, your mom or your dad. Ask God to forgive you…and then apologize to the person you hurt and ask for forgiveness. What can we do to keep from destruction with our words?

- Commandment 7 tells us not to commit adultery. "Committing adultery" means not being loyal to your husband or wife. Maybe you've had a friend who wasn't loyal to you. What did you feel when suddenly he or she wasn't your friend anymore? Why does Jesus want us to be loyal friends to one another?

- "You shall not steal," reads Commandment 8. Have you ever had anything stolen from you? How did you feel? Why doesn't Jesus want us to steal?

- Commandment 9 tells us not to lie. When, if ever, has someone lied about you or to you? Did you feel angry? Helpless? Frustrated? Hurt? All of these things? Think about a time when you told a lie to someone. Why did you do that? What—or Who—can keep you from lying next time?

- Commandment 10 means that we shouldn't be wanting what other people own. When have you wanted what someone else had and you finally got it only to realize it wasn't all that cool? In what ways did wanting that something change your relationship with the person who owned it?

Not destroying with our words, not being disloyal, not stealing, not lying, and not being jealous of other people—the last five commandments, like the first five, are not easy to obey if we don't have God's help

Now here's your shortcut!—again straight from Jesus Himself. He says, "And the second is like it: 'Love your neighbor as yourself'" (Matthew 22:39). If you treat other people the way you want them to treat you (yep, that's the Golden Rule!), you'll find yourself automatically obeying six of the Ten Commandments! Is it loving to murder? To steal? To lie? Would you want someone stealing from you or lying about you? So if you follow the Golden Rule and treat folks the way you want them to treat you, you'll be obeying Commandments 6–10!

Have you ever noticed that being told not to do something can make us want to do that very thing? Since that's the case, rewrite these six commandments so that they're positive commands. Number 10, for instance, could become "Be thankful for all that God has given you."

Commandments… rules… "Thou shalt nots…" They hardly sound good for us, but they are. Think of the laws as being like a kite string. Can a kite fly without being attached to a string? A kite only knows its freedom in the wind because it's attached to a string. Likewise, we only know freedom in Jesus and His love when we stay attached and obedient to his laws.

Draw a Commandment

Have a poster contest. See who can creatively illustrate one of God's commandments. Set a time limit and then let the contest begin!

1. Appoint three or four people to serve as judges. Be sure that the panel includes children and teens as well as adults.
2. Send invitations to the "gallery showing." (Be sure to include the time, place, and date of the showing. Also let guests know when the contest winners will be announced.)
3. Display the finished posters in a large room or in your backyard.
4. When people arrive, invite them to enjoy refreshments and browse through the gallery. Encourage them to pay close attention to workmanship, symbolism, creativity, and content.
5. When the judges have decided on the winners, ask everyone to sit down for the awarding of prizes.

You may want to give prizes for:
- Most creative
- Best workmanship
- Best illustration of a commandment's meaning

Prizes can be a trip to the winner's favorite ice cream parlor or a $5 gift certificate to a great local Christian bookstore. Use your imagination—and have fun!

A Chain of Commands

1. Take an 8½-x-11-inch sheet of colored construction paper and cut it lengthwise into ten equal strips. Write one of the Ten Commandments from Exodus 20 on each strip.
2. Make a circle of the First Commandment strip by gluing or taping the ends together.
3. Link the next commandment strip through the first and glue or tape its ends together.
4. Continue until all ten strips are linked together to form a chain.
5. Hang the chain on your bedpost or from a peg on the wall of your room.
6. As you read the Bible and find more of God's commandments, add links to your chain. Think about how the strength of the chain depends on the strength of each link, just as the strength of our moral character depends on our keeping each of God's commandments.

MINING GOD'S WORD FOR ITS TREASURES

What do you think of when you hear the word _unique_? One of a kind? Nothing else like it? Something to be treasured? Something not to be ignored?

The Bible is all this—and much, much more! It is Holy Spirit–inspired, and every single verse can teach us or correct us....

> All Scripture is Godbreathed and is useful for teaching, rebuking, correcting and training in righteousness....
>
> 2 Timothy 3:16

Its teachings can keep us from sinning against God...

> For the word of the LORD is right and true; he is faithful in all he does.
>
> Psalm 33:4

It directs our steps...

> Your word is a lamp to my feet and a light for my path.
>
> Psalm 119:105

It guides our actions...

> The man who looks intently into the perfect law that gives freedom, and continues to do this, not forgetting what he has heard, but doing it—he will be blessed in what he does.
>
> James 1:25

It is light and truth in a very dark world...

> "You are the light of the world. A city on a hill cannot be hidden. Let your light shine before men, that they may see your good deeds and praise your Father in heaven."
>
> Matthew 5:14, 16

In this section you'll learn about some other unique aspects of the Bible. May what you learn encourage you to read God's Word and discover treasures that will bless your life for now and always!

The Basics of the Bible

Knowing some basic facts about a letter—who wrote it and when and why—can make that letter much more interesting and meaningful! Well, the Bible—a collection of sixty-six letters and books—is no different. It's much more interesting and much more fun to read God's Book when we know some basic facts about it!

Okay, let the learning about Bible basics begin!

THE BIBLE IS DIVIDED INTO TWO MAJOR PARTS

The Old Testament…the books written *before* Jesus walked the earth.

The New Testament…the books written *after* Jesus' life, death, and resurrection.

Testament means "covenant" or "agreement," so *Old Testament* simply means God's old agreement with His people. God told them how they should live under the law that He had given them through Moses. *New Testament* means God's new agreement, and in those twenty-seven books He teaches people how to live under grace once they know Jesus Christ as their Savior and Lord.

The Old Testament is much more about *doing*—more specifically, the things *God* wants us to do (outward actions); the New Testament is more about *being*—the condition of our heart and mind (inward actions). The message of the New Testament shows us God cares about both our doing *and* our being. We act according to who we are, what we think, and how we feel about ourselves, other people and things. And God, by the power of the Holy Spirit, wants us to be more like Jesus and more able to act like Him!

THE OLD TESTAMENT CONTAINS FIVE KINDS OF BOOKS

Law Books: The first five books of the Bible—Genesis through Deuteronomy—are the books of God's law. These are the rules God gave people to bring order into our lives. The rules tell us how we should treat one another and live together in community.

History Books: These twelve books tell the roller-coaster history of the nation of Israel as they follow God, fall away from God, repent and turn to God, follow God, fall away from God…. You get the picture.

Poetry Collections: The book of Psalms is the Bible's hymnbook; Job, Proverbs, and Ecclesiastes are considered the Bible's wisdom literature; and Song of Solomon celebrates love.

Major Prophets: Isaiah, Jeremiah, and Ezekiel faithfully reported—in lengthy books (Jeremiah wrote two!)—what God told them would happen in the future, especially if they did not obey His laws! Daniel is also included in this grouping.

Minor Prophets: "Minor" only in length and not in importance, these twelve books also talk about God's plans for His people's future. These books also outline what would happen if God's people did or did not obey the rules God gave us to keep us from destroying ourselves and each other.

THE NEW TESTAMENT ALSO HAS FIVE KINDS OF BOOKS

The Gospels: Four different writers—Matthew, Mark, Luke, and John—report the real truth about what Jesus did and said while He was here on earth. Each of these four described Jesus' life from his own special viewpoint.

History Book—Acts: Dr. Luke offers a carefully researched and accurate account of what happened to the new believers after the resurrected Jesus returned to heaven to be with His Father.

Paul's Letters: Paul wrote these letters to encourage and teach new believers as the church grew and the gospel was shared throughout the known world.

General Letters: Other believers wrote these letters to encourage fellow Christians in their walk with the Lord and to let them know what God was doing to build His kingdom on earth.

The Book of Prophecy—Revelation: John, the apostle and friend of Jesus who loved Him so much, wrote this last book of the Bible to encourage believers and to tell them what would happen between Satan and God at the end of time.

A Look Into Literature

OLD TESTAMENT

LAW BOOKS

HISTORY BOOKS

POETRY COLLECTION

MAJOR PROPHETS

MINOR PROPHETS

NEW TESTAMENT

THE GOSPELS

HISTORY BOOKS

PAUL'S LETTERS

GENERAL LETTERS

PROPHECY

On ten different slips of paper, write down the following:

- **Kinds of Books** (one of the following on each slip of paper):

* Law books	* The Gospels
* History books I	* History books II
* Poetry collections	* Paul's letters
* Major prophets	* General letters
* Minor prophets	* Book of prophecy—Revelation

- **Old or New Testament?**
- **When?**
- **What?**

Place the slips in a container and shake them up. At the end of this family time, have folks each draw a piece of paper out of the container.

First, have each person identify whether the collection listed is in the Old Testament or the New. (If any other details are offered, that person could receive two chocolate dipped strawberries!)

Next, explain when the collection was written in relation to Jesus' life.

Finally, depending upon when the collection was written, state whether it fell under the old agreement (life under the law) or the new agreement (life under grace).

Anyone who answers every item correctly gets a pint of strawberries with dipping chocolate! Younger family members get an extra berry for trying.

Sixty-Six Books, One Cover

Duplicate this drawing and put it in your Bible or on your bedroom wall. It's a great tool for helping you learn—and remember—the kind of book you are reading whenever you open God's Word.

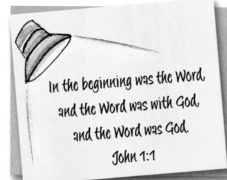

In the beginning was the Word
and the Word was with God,
and the Word was God.

John 1:1

What Version Is It?

Did you know that the Bible was originally written in Hebrew and Greek? Did you know that getting the Bible translated into English cost some people their lives? And did you know that, even today, in some places around the world believers don't have a Bible to read?

You probably have more than one Bible in your house, and you may have several different translations. Today there are many versions of the Bible available to us. The oldest one is the King James Version, which dates back to 1611. Some of the more popular modern versions of the Bible are the New International Version (NIV), the New American Standard Bible (NASB), New Living Translation (NLT), and the Revised Standard Version (RSV). Paraphrases like the *New Living Bible* and *The Message* by Eugene Peterson are also widely read. There are picture-book story Bibles for young children, easy-to-read Bibles for kindergarteners and first graders, and youth Bibles for older kids. And of course there are Bibles with extras that are targeted for men or women, teenagers or seminary students, singles or couples. The list goes on and on!

So how do you decide which Bible to call your own? Browse a Christian bookstore and talk to the Bible expert there. Or, in the comfort of your own home, log onto the Internet's Bible Gateway (www.biblegateway.com). There you can read and compare your favorite verses in a variety of translations and see what you like best. Whichever Bible you settle on, don't let dust settle on it! After all, "man does not live on bread alone but on every word that comes from the mouth of the LORD" (Deuteronomy 8:3).

Bible Scramble

YOU WILL NEED:

- 78 three-by-five-inch index cards
- Four different-colored markers
- Box of paper clips
- Ball of kite string that will work like a clothesline
- Bible

Use a marker to label one index card "Old Testament" and another "New Testament."

Next, using a different-colored marker, label ten more index cards with the division of the Bible: Law, History, Poetry, Major Prophets, Minor Prophets, Gospels, History, Paul's Letters, General Letters, and New Testament Prophecy. Use a third marker to write the name of each of the Old Testament books on separate index cards; and use a fourth color to write the name of each of the New Testament books on separate index cards.

TABLE SCRAMBLE

1. Place the two "Old Testament" and "New Testament" cards on a table. Next, mix up the ten cards that are labeled with the divisions of the Bible. Use a timer and take turns to see who can put the ten cards in order under "Old Testament" and "New Testament" before the timer runs out. As you get better, shorten the time allowed.
2. Next, try racing the timer by putting the books of the Old Testament in order.
3. Finally, see how long it takes to put the books of the New Testament in order.

CLOTHESLINE SCRAMBLE

Stretch a clothesline or thin cord between two trees in the backyard or across an archway or garage door opening.

1. Lay all of the cards faceup on a table, the sidewalk, or the driveway.
2. On your mark, get set, go! Using paper clips, hang the cards on the line in the correct order. Intersperse the division cards where they belong between the book cards. (In other words, "Paul's Letters" should go after "Acts" and before "Romans.") Use a stopwatch to see who finishes in the least amount of time—and be sure to give the timekeeper a chance to play!

Who Wrote It...To You?

Someone once described the Bible as God's love letter to us! Now, a letter—especially one in which the writer proclaims his love—is a very personal form of communication. And the Bible is indeed a very personal message from God to us. To make this fact a little more real, do the following exercise with some of the Scripture passages your family is learning. If you own a copy of *The Message*, you'll find an introduction to each book of the Bible. These introductions (and other translations have similar sections) contain great information about the writer and an overview of what he intended us to learn.

1. Find out *who* wrote the Bible verses and to *whom* the message was originally written.
2. Discuss what the Scripture passage means to your family today.
3. Then write the Bible verses in the form of a letter addressed to someone in your family. (Some books in the New Testament *are* letters; they're called epistles.)
4. Mail your rewritten Bible verses to each other.

You might even send one of these Bible letters to friends or try answering the letters in the Bible with letters to the authors. Whatever you do, you're sure to come to a greater understanding of God's Word.

SAMPLE BIBLE LETTER (based on Ephesians 1:15–19):

Dear Molly,

Ever since I heard about your faith in the Lord Jesus and your love for all the saints, I have not stopped giving thanks for you, remembering you in my prayers. I keep asking that the God of our Lord Jesus Christ, the glorious Father, may give you the Spirit of wisdom and revelation, so that you may know Him better.

I pray also that the eyes of your heart may be enlightened in order that you may know the hope to which He has called you.

Peace and blessings to you,

Paul

"Who Said It?" Bingo

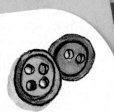

1. Make bingo cards that are five squares across and five squares down. Draw a Bible in the "free square" in the center.

2. In each square, write the name of a Bible character given by the game leader. Each player should write the names on their cards in different arrangements. Use a Bible dictionary or the index at the back of your Bible for ideas.

3. Give each player a handful of beans, buttons, or pennies to use as markers.

4. The first player will quote a Bible character (or offer a paraphrase of a Bible character's words), ask, "Who said it?" and then choose someone to answer. If the person chosen knows the answer, he or she covers that Bible character's name square on the bingo card. The player to the left of the one who just asked the question (yes, you're moving clockwise around the circle!) will say the next quote.

5. Variation:
   - A game leader can list quotes from the Bible characters and read a different quote each time.
   - Any player can raise a hand to answer "Who said it?"
   - Anyone who has that Bible character's name on his or her card can cover the square.
   - Players win when they cover one row of squares—down, across, or diagonally.

SAMPLE PARAPHRASES:

- "Are you absolutely sure there is no room in the inn?" (Luke 2:7)
- "I said it is definitely time to get on board! Don't push! Just two at a time." (Genesis 7:6–9)
- "The seventh time around is a charm, they say." (Joshua 6:2–5)
- "I want to do good, but every time I try, I just mess up." (Romans 7:15)
- "Yes, let those children come right over here and see Me." (Matthew 19:14)

AN AMAZING INVITATION

Don't you love being invited to a birthday party? It means friends and fun, ice cream and cake, gifts and goody bags, and often piñatas and games. You read the invitation and run to the calendar. You don't want to miss out on this grand event!

Well, there's an even more exciting invitation that comes to you and me in the Bible, and it's to a grand and eternal event that you definitely want to be part of. The invitation is from God, and He wants us to recognize His love for us and choose to return that love. God's love is most obvious in the gift of His Son, Jesus Christ, who died on the cross as punishment for our sins (John 3:16; Romans 5:8). When we recognize our sins, we realize what an amazing gift that is and, in an act of love and thanksgiving, name Jesus as our Savior and Lord. That decision is the foundation for an exciting and lifelong relationship with God. And you don't want to miss out on that!

You are forgiving and good, O Lord, abounding in love to all who call to you.

Psalm 86:5

Love the Lord with All Your Heart

Think about your heart.

Now, when you read that sentence, you probably think of your physical heart, that blood-pumping muscle inside your chest. But there is also your emotional heart, that part of you with which you experience feelings. Sometimes you have a happy heart, and at other times your heart feels sad.

In the Bible the word *heart* usually means that place of feelings or the center of your very personhood. Look at these verses about the heart:

Deuteronomy 30:14–16

Psalm 26:2

Proverbs 15:13–15

Mark 12:30

Luke 2:19; 6:45

Acts 2:46

For the word of the Lord is right and true; He is faithful in all He does.

Psalm 33:4

Here I am! I stand at the door and knock. If anyone hears my voice and opens the door, I will come in....

Revelation 3:20

WHAT DOES IT MEAN TO "INVITE JESUS INTO YOUR HEART"?

Inviting Jesus into your heart is a lot like inviting someone into your home. Usually you think about all the people you invite and why you want them to visit. Sometimes you send a written invitation. Then, before they come, you plan your time so that, once they arrive, you can visit with them and enjoy their company. Often you share your feelings with them. And friends you welcome into your home are the type of friends who will help you when you need help. Good friendships like that last through the years and bring great joy to life.

INVITE JESUS TO BE YOUR FRIEND

1. Think about why you want Jesus to be your Friend.
2. Write out an invitation and ask Jesus to be with you.
3. Plan the time you will spend with Jesus every day.
4. What feelings or needs do you want to share with Him?

Jesus wants to be your Best Friend for life. So invite Him into your heart, the center of your being.

He can turn a sad heart into a happy heart!

The Transformed Life

When you give your life to Jesus, your heart changes…your actions change…your life changes. You are a new person!

A Vivid—and Tasty—Picture of God's Transforming Work!

Popcorn offers a great illustration of the transformation Christ works in your life.

Unpopped Kernels ~ Before people become Christians, their hearts are hard and their lives unusable for God's kingdom work (Ephesians 4:18).

Multicolored Kernels ~ Jesus died for all people regardless of the color of their skin (Acts 10:34–35).

Oil ~ This represents the Holy Spirit, who convicts us of our sin and makes us feel sorry for dissappointing things we've done (John 16:8, ESV).

Pan ~ The pan enables the popcorn to become edible (that's what it's supposed to be!). Likewise, God's family helps us become all God wants us to be (Ephesians 3:20–21).

Heat ~ The flame represents the fire of the Lord's passionate and life-changing love for us (2 Timothy 1:6, ESV).

Popped Corn ~ Now, wearing the white of a wedding dress, popcorn symbolizes a life turned completely inside out and our readiness to be the bride of Christ (Revelation 19:7–8).

Salt ~ We are the salt of the earth (Matthew 5:13).

No Pepper ~ We need to avoid those things that can make us unclean and impure (2 Timothy 2:22).

Kernels That Won't Pop ~ Kernels that do not pop are like people who refuse to come to Christ (John 3:36).

Why not make some delicious, white, fluffy popcorn for a snack right now? As you share it with your family, share, too, how the Lord is able to use you since He changed your heart and life. (Sometimes it's hard for us to see how God is using us. So take this opportunity to let each other know how you see God using each other in your life, in the lives of other family members, and even outside the home.)

We...are being transformed into his likeness with everincreasing glory, which comes from the Lord, who is the Spirit.
2 Corinthians 3:18

Let the "Life Saver" Save Your Life—for Eternity

If you were on a boat and a man fell overboard, what could you do? You could jump in the water and try to save him, or you could throw him a life preserver. This lifesaving tool is a buoyant device, usually in the shape of a ring, designed to keep a person afloat in the water. It is tied to a lifeline that is securely fastened to the boat so the person can be pulled to safety.

THE COLORS OF CANDY LIFESAVERS CAN REMIND US OF JESUS, OUR "LIFE SAVER."

 RED stands for the blood of Jesus, shed on the cross for you and me (1 John 1:7).

 WHITE is for the way Jesus' death and resurrection makes us clean when we accept that he did this for *us* (Psalm 51:7).

 GREEN is for the new heart-growth that comes when we spend time with Jesus praying and reading his love letters to us (the Bible), and worshiping together with other believers (Psalm 1:2–3).

 YELLOW is for the "streets of gold" we'll see when we get to our heavenly home (Revelation 21:21).

ORANGE is for "Orange you glad you have a *real* Life Saver in your heart?"

At the pool or the beach, lifesavers—buoys, tubes, hooks, and ropes—are meant to be shared with people who need them! Likewise, our knowledge of our Life Saver—Jesus Christ—is meant to be shared. Jesus wants to help people who are drowning in sin, discouragement, or loneliness. He wants to help people who are feeling crushed by waves of hopelessness and purposelessness. He wants to save them now and for eternity. So think about folks you know. Who needs your Life Saver now?

A Growth Chart for the Heart

Measurements of our weight and height indicate our physical growth. Tests during our years of school indicate our educational growth. But how do we know if we are growing spiritually? God's Word says we will grow spiritually if we obey God's instructions and love one another. We'll have an easier time obeying God's Word if we know—really know—what it says, so let's memorize some Scripture as well as do some other things that will both encourage and reflect our growth in the Lord.

A word of caution: Marking a chart whenever we do something which pleases the Lord is not to make us proud of ourselves. Instead we are to feel thankful for God's grace in our lives—for the grace of being called to know Him as our heavenly Father, for the freedom to own a Bible in a language we understand so we can learn His truths, for the Holy Spirit who helps us become the people God wants us to be! To get started, memorize the three verses we've provided. List them in the "Memorize Scripture" column of your chart (instructions for making one are on the following page) and then color in three sections on your measuring strip.

See that you go on growing in the Lord
and become strong and vigorous
in the truth you were taught.
Colossians 2:7, TLB

And Jesus grew in wisdom and stature,
and in favor with God and men.
Luke 2:52

Grow in the grace and knowledge of our
Lord and Savior Jesus Christ.
To him be glory both now and forever!
2 Peter 3:18

- Using a sheet of poster board, make a "Growth Chart for the Heart." Moving from left to right, label sections as follows:
  - * Ask for God's Guidance
  - * Recognize and Avoid Doing Wrong
  - * Help Someone
  - * Memorize Scripture
  - * Follow Jesus' Example
  - * Feel Thankful
- Hang the chart on your bedroom wall. Make an entry in the appropriate section each time you remember to do one of the things on your chart and write down a corresponding Bible verse; then record them in the "Memorize Scripture" column of your chart. Color in three sections on your measuring strip.
- Next, hang on your bedroom or bathroom wall a strip of paper that is as long as you are tall. Divide the strip into one- or two-inch sections. Each time you record an entry on your chart, color in a section of your measuring strip with a marker or crayon. (Be careful of the wall!) Think about using a different color for each of the six categories on your chart.

This is what God the LORD says—
he who created the heavens and stretched them out,
who spread out the
earth and all that comes out of it,
who gives breath to its people,
and life to those who walk on it:
"I, the LORD, have called you in righteousness;
I will take hold of your hand."

Isaiah 42:5—6

God is our heavenly Father. He is also our best friend. He loves us more than we can ever comprehend. He loves us even before we please Him; He loves us when we disobey.

He is an awesome God. He has such incredible power that just by speaking into empty space He caused everything in this entire galaxy—and in all other galaxies as well—to come into existence. Single words from His mouth made the sky, the oceans, the mountains, the rivers, the plants, the animals, the birds, the fish, the insects, and finally us! Without Him we wouldn't even *be!*

For this reason alone, our Creator God deserves our honor and respect. In fact, such reverence for God is absolutely necessary if our lives are to exemplify Him and the blessings He gives us. Our reverence for God must therefore be our motivation, guide, goal, and focus in everything we do.

Before anything else existed, there was God. When everything stops existing, there will still be God. In this section we will share some ways to live with a respect for this eternal, omnipotent, omniscient, and truly amazing God.

What's in a Name?

Our names are very important to our identities. Most of us have names that were carefully chosen by our parents. But we have other names, too, that tell something about us. For example, your name may be Benjamin, which means "much beloved and favored son." But you could also bear the names of "friend," "brother," "son," "grandson," "nephew," "third baseman," "student," "drummer."

God's name is very important, but in the beginning people considered it too holy to be spoken out loud. They simply wrote *YHWH*, a name that meant "I AM THAT I AM" and that pointed to the faithfulness and unchangeableness of God. When the ancient Jews came across *YHWH*, they would substitute their word for "my Lord" in its place. When the vowels from that word were added to *YHWH*, the name *Jehovah* resulted.

Scripture also gives God other names that describe His character and identify His qualities. Names like those listed below show our God to be all-sufficient, totally able to meet every need we have. Read through these names of God found in Scripture and the meaning of, or quality associated with, each name:

Jehovah Jireh ~ The Lord Provides
Jehovah Rapha ~ The Lord That Heals
El Shaddai ~ The All-Sufficient One
El Roi ~ God Who Sees
Elohim ~ The Creator
Adonai ~ Lord, Master
Jehovah Shalom ~ The Lord Is Peace
El Olam ~ The Everlasting God
Jehovah Raah ~ The Lord My Shepherd

Jehovah Sabaoth ~ The Lord of Hosts
Jehovah Tsidkenu ~ The Lord Our Righteousness
El Elyon ~ The God Most High
Emmanuel ~ God with Us
Wonderful Counselor
Redeemer

1. Buy self-adhesive name tags or labels.
2. Give several labels to each member of your family. On one label have everyone write his or her "main name" with a black marker.
3. Then, using different colors of markers, make name tags that reflect all the other names each person might have ("aunt," "driver," "dad," "teacher," "horseback rider," etc.).
4. Now give each person several more name tags on which to write God's main name and His other names, such as "El Roi—God Who Sees," "Jehovah Rapha—The Lord That Heals," "Jehovah Shalom—The Lord is Peace," etc.
5. Think together of the needs your family has that would be met by each quality of God. Does your family face a big decision? Know that God is your Counselor. Does someone in your family need physical, emotional, or even spiritual healing? Know that God is the Great Physician. Do uncertain finances make you feel as if you're standing on shifting sand? Turn to God, your Rock.
6. Keep your name tags for God close at hand. When you face a particular problem, write it down on a sheet of paper or in your prayer journal. Then glance through the name tags. Next to your entry, write the name of God that is most encouraging to you in this situation.
7. Now, as you pray together, focus on God's promise to be all and exactly what we need, whatever our need is.

And remember…

My God will meet all your needs according to his glorious riches in Christ Jesus.
Philippians 4:19

Have you bought enough magazines, gift wrap, and candy in support of your kids' schools? Are the cars clean, the grass cut, and the garage organized—but your kids still want to earn some money? Try this alternative fund-raising idea!

1. Donate ten dollars for every Christian biography your children or grandchildren read and discuss with you.

2. After each biography has been read, discuss that person's life with your reader. What statement could summarize his passion or goals? What attitude characterized her life? What hardships did he endure—and how did God redeem them? What blessings did she experience as she served the Lord? Then choose a Scripture verse that epitomizes that person's life and memorize it together.

3. Use brightly colored tape to mark the spine of each book you read. On the tape use a marker to write down the Scripture reference you memorized.

4. Let your children choose special causes or organizations that they feel can really make a difference. Encourage them to donate all or a portion of their "book earnings."

5. Talk about other ways each of us, beginning at a very early age, can make a difference for the kingdom of God.

When your students are on a reading program like this, people like John Wesley, David Livingstone, and Corrie ten Boom will become their heroes, and their love for reading will also increase. They will also be supporting their favorite cause—helping them grow as Christians. You can't put a price on that!

Let us consider how we may spur one another on toward love and good deeds.
Hebrews 10:24

Honoring God's Book

Have you ever stopped to consider what an amazing gift the Bible is? In its pages we learn about God, His great love for us, His plan for our salvation, and so much more! May we never take for granted that precious Book!

Think together about what your family can do to honor the Bible. Children and adults alike need to respect the Scriptures because its words are indeed God's life-giving truth.

- Keep the Bible out on a table or nightstand where people can see it and pick it up throughout the day.
- Take along a Bible whenever your family goes on a trip. (Many travel-size editions are available.)
- Reading the Bible often will help keep it dust free. But when your family returns from vacation, be sure to dust off the Bible and get back in the habit of opening it daily.
- Never pile magazines, newspapers, or other books on top of a Bible. After all, its words are the supreme authority for our lives, so—to represent that fact—nothing should ever be placed on top of it.
- Choose for each of your children a version of the Bible that is appropriate for their age, reading ability, and maturity level.
- Teach children to hold the Bible carefully and to never tear its pages or mishandle it in any way. Try not to drop it and never set drinks or food on it.
- Keep a copy of the Bible in your car to read when you are stuck in traffic or find yourself waiting for someone.
- Both Mom and Dad should have their own copy of the Bible so that children will see them reading Scripture and learn early that it is our God-given guide for daily living.

Read the Bible together as a family as often as possible. Breakfast, dinnertime, and bedtime are three options.

- What truths from God's Word can give you hope or peace when you're afraid?
- What verses from the Bible can help you say no to temptation and sin?
- What if someone asks you to explain why you believe your sins are forgiven?

In these three situations—and many, many others—God's Word can give us *exactly* what we need.

In fact, God's Spirit can bring to mind the truth that will help us in the moment, but we can give Him more to work with if we've memorized Scripture. So just do it!

And know that you're never too young or too old to hide God's Word in your heart. It's spiritual nourishment that just can't be beat!

"Man does not live on bread alone, but on every word that comes from the mouth of God."

Matthew 4:4

Daily Fun with God's Word
Cheri Steinbrinck

"**Our two-year-old, Ellen,** has an excellent memory, and we have 'Bible verse time' every day." Here is the plan Ellen's mother, Cheri, uses with her:

- ❤ Read the whole verse, stating the reference at both the beginning and the end.
- ❤ Recite a few words at a time and let the child repeat them phrase by phrase until you have worked through the verse.
- ❤ Play "fill in the blank." Start by leaving out one word, then two, and so on until the child learns the entire verse.
- ❤ Aim toward having the child say the verse alone by the end of the week.
- ❤ Review the Bible verse often during the everyday activities of the week.

"Lord, Make Me Clean"

Most of us take a shower or a bath every day! It's good to be clean, isn't it? When we are really dirty, we take for granted that we will have hot water, a bar of soap (or maybe even bubble bath), and fresh, clean towels. Those are the things we need to feel clean and be clean on the outside! (When was the last time you said, "Thank You, Lord, for soap and water"?)

The Bible talks about the importance of being clean on the *inside*. When our hearts are full of sin, we can feel dirty and sad, but the blood of Jesus— and only the blood of Jesus—can wash our hearts clean. The psalmist David prayed, "Wash me, and I will be whiter than snow" (Psalm 51:7). God loves to answer prayers like that!

Let us draw near to God with a sincere heart
in full assurance of faith,
having our hearts sprinkled to cleanse us
from a guilty conscience and
having our bodies washed with pure water.

Hebrews 10:22

MAKE SHOWER VERSE CARDS

1. On five-by-seven-inch index cards, write out some of the verses we've provided below.
2. Laminate the cards. (Clear self-adhesive shelf paper will work, and lamination sheets are available at most office supply stores.)
3. Punch a hole in the cards, string them together with kite string or yarn, and hang the collection in the shower or bathtub.
4. Have a new card face up each week.
5. Quiz one another at breakfast or dinner on the week's verse and talk about what it means.

- Matthew 8:2
- Titus 3:5
- Psalm 51:2, NLT
- Hebrews 10:22
- Psalm 119:9, NLT
- Acts 22:16
- Isaiah 1:16, 25
- 1 Corinthians 6:11, NLT
- Ephesians 5:25–27, NLT
- 1 John 1:7, 9

Wash me, and I'll be whiter than snow.
Psalm 51:7

A Little Friendly Competition

There is only one kind of competition encouraged in the Bible. Do you know what it is? The Bible encourages us to outdo each other in serving and loving each other (Matthew 7:12). Here's a fun family contest to see how many Scripture verses each of you can learn. Let's see what "events" God's Word outlines for this competition! We'll look up verses that tell us how to serve and love each other, then we'll memorize them. But always remember what's most important of all—*doing* them!

When we participate in a little friendly competition to hide God's Word in our hearts, *no one* ever loses!

Scripture Memory Challenge

Where: Family Room

When: Sunday 4:00

PRIZES! PRIZES!

> I have hidden your word in my heart that I might not sin against you.
>
> Psalm 119:11

1. Choose a week to review and memorize a predetermined number of Bible verses, based upon the ages of the children participating.
2. Collect an assortment of small prizes that you know will be a hit with your family members and one "grand prize" for the winner—e.g., a homemade coupon/gift certificate for a favorite treat or service.
3. During the competition the first person recites a verse. Each person must then recite a different verse.
4. If a person can't recite a verse that has not already been recited, that person is out.
5. Keep score of how many verses each person recites and award a daily winner. Give a double score to younger players.
6. Add up each person's score for the week and award the grand prize to the person who memorized the most verses.

Alphabetical Bible Collection

- Buy everyone in the family an inexpensive address book.
- Record in alphabetical order by the first word those Bible verses you want to learn.

  For example:

  > D—"Delight yourself also in the LORD, and He shall give you the desires of your heart" (Psalm 37:4, NKJV).
  >
  > F—"Follow me, and I will make you fishers of men" (Matthew 4:19, ESV).

- Carry your Bible alphabet book with you when you have to be away at camp or college, on vacation or a business trip, or in the military. Your book will give you quick and easy-to-access encouragement and godly wisdom in new situations. Having God's Word with you will enrich your days and lift your spirits if you run into problems.
- On family trips, use these Bible alphabet books to play the Alphabet Race Game. The first person recites an *A* verse, the next person says a *B* verse, and so on until you've gone through the entire alphabet.

The Alphabet Race Game is a good opportunity for people to add verses to their books.

And it might be fun to award a prize whenever someone has a verse for every letter from A to Z. Of course, finding verses that begin with the letters Q, X, and Z might prove challenging, so you may consider a "bonus" prize for those!

Medicine for a Healthy Spirit

Did you know that doctors have determined that the attitudes of our heart directly affect the health of our body? Here are some of the connections they've noticed:

ATTITUDES	DISEASES
Anger	Ulcers
Frustration	Stress on the heart
Worry	Circulatory disease
Stress	Headaches
Guilt and resentment	Eating disorders
Holding grudges	Sleeplessness

This may be one reason why God's Word has a lot to say to us about keeping our spirits and attitudes healthy. So try this way of internalizing God's "vitamins"! As His Word builds healthy attitudes, you may be building a strong body as well.

1. Type or write on small strips of paper some of God's healthy instructive verses (a list follows). Roll each of the strips up tightly and tie with a ribbon.
2. Put the scrolls in a small box and place it on your nightstand next to your bed.
3. Each night before going to sleep, be sure to take a "vitamin" out of your box. Open the scroll, read the verse several times, and think about what it really means.
4. Pray about what God is trying to say to you as it applies to your life.
5. Go to sleep thinking about God's good words instead of anything from the day that may have caused you anger, frustration, or stress.

A heart at peace gives life to the body.
Proverbs 14:30

HERE ARE SOME DOSES OF SPIRITUAL MEDICINE:

- "My God will meet all your needs according to his glorious riches in Christ Jesus" (Philippians 4:19).

- "The precepts of the LORD are right, giving joy to the heart. The commands of the LORD are radiant, giving light to the eyes" (Psalm 19:8).

- "We have peace with God through our Lord Jesus Christ, through whom we have gained access by faith into this grace in which we now stand" (Romans 5:1–2).

- "My grace is sufficient for you, for my power is made perfect in weakness" (2 Corinthians 12:9).

- "For God has not given us a spirit of fear, but of power and of love and of a sound mind" (2 Timothy 1:7, NKJV).

- "'For I know the plans I have for you,' declares the LORD, 'plans to prosper you and not to harm you, plans to give you hope and a future'" (Jeremiah 29:11).

Have you ever wished that your kids came with an owner's manual? Well, they do. It's called the Bible—and their Creator and Owner and heavenly Father gave it to us parents so we know how to raise the children He entrusts to our care. Among the instructions we find there, God is very clear that we are to point our kids to Him, to teach them His truth, and to instruct them in His ways.

In Deuteronomy 6, we see that this responsibility is a 24/7 job. Wherever we are and wherever we go, whatever we're doing and whatever we're looking at—everything can cue us to teach about God, praise Him, thank Him, or pray to Him. Before you know it, both generations will be more aware of God's gracious presence with us and His amazing love for us.

These commandments that I give you today are to be upon your hearts. Impress them on your children. Talk about them when you sit at home and when you walk along the road, when you lie down and when you get up. Tie them as symbols on your hands and bind them on your foreheads. Write them on the doorframes of your houses and on your gates.

Deuteronomy 6:6–9

Live the way the Lord your God has commanded you so that you may live and have what is good and have a long life in the land you will take.... You, your children, and your grandchildren must respect the LORD your God as long as you live. Obey all his rules and commands I give you so that you will live a long time. Listen, Israel, carefully obey these laws. Then all will go well for you, and you will become a great nation in a fertile land, just as the LORD, the God of your ancestors, has promised you. Listen, people of Israel. The LORD our God is the only LORD. Love the LORD your God with all your heart, all your soul, and all your strength. Always remember these commands I give you today. Teach them to your children and talk about them when you sit at home and walk along the road. When you lie down and when you get up. Write them down and tie them on your hands as a sign. Tie them on your forehead to remind you, write them on your doors and gates.

Deuteronomy 5:33, 6:2–9 (paraphrased)

When You Lie Down...

Did you know that the ideas and words that are in our minds when we lie down for the night are likely to stay with us? These thoughts may work in our subconscious as we sleep and dream, and when we awaken again, these same ideas may be a part of our conscious thought patterns. That being the case, what better time could there be to store God's Word in our hearts than when we lie down?

In this chapter you will find activities to help you think about good things before you go to sleep so that you will rest more peacefully. In fact, when you calm your mind and close your day by thinking on God's truth, you will experience the truth of His promise to "keep him in perfect peace, whose mind is stayed on thee" (Isaiah 26:3, ASV). Sweet dreams!

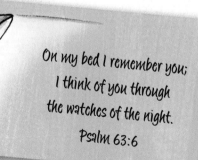

On my bed I remember you;
I think of you through
the watches of the night.
Psalm 63:6

Promise Pillow

Do you have a favorite pillow? There's nothing better than curling up with that pillow before you fall asleep, is there? Well, before turning out the lights at bedtime, why not use your pillow to help you fill your mind with a promise of God's care and faithfulness?

- Make or buy a small satin or soft flannel pillow. Sew a pocket to one side of the pillow.
- On strips of paper that will fit into that pocket when they're folded, write these verses that speak comforting assurance about God's presence with you and love for you. Choose one verse to learn each week. Read it several times every evening. Then fold it up and tuck it into the pocket of your Promise Pillow.
- By the end of the week, you will know the verse by heart! Tape the memorized verse on your bedroom door so that you'll see these bedtime promises each night as you enter your room.

When you lie down,
you will not be afraid;
when you lie down,
your sleep will be sweet.
Proverbs 3:24

When you lie down,
you will not be afraid;
When you lie down, your sleep will be sweet.

Proverbs 3:24

CHOOSE A NEW VERSE AT THE BEGINNING OF EACH WEEK:

Psalm 91:11	1 John 5:14–15	Jeremiah 17:7–8
Proverbs 3:24	John 14:1	John 14:13–14
Psalm 121:1–2	John 14:27	Philippians 4:8
Psalm 121:3–4	Psalm 23:6	1 Peter 5:6–7
Psalm 121:5–6	Isaiah 41:10	Philippians 4:13
Psalm 121:7–8	Romans 8:38–39	1 Thessalonians 5:8

Angel Watch

Matthew 18:10 tells us that children have angels that watch over them and give account to (and always have the attention of) God Himself. Jesus said, "See that you do not look down on one of these little ones. For I tell you that their angels in heaven always see the face of my Father in heaven."

JUST WHAT DO ANGELS *DO* WITH THEIR TIME?

- ♥ They bring messages
- ♥ They stand guard
- ♥ They protect
- ♥ They warn
- ♥ They go before us to make a way
- ♥ They dispel fear
- ♥ They prevent disaster

1. Choose a different-colored 8-x-11-inch poster board for each of the functions listed above. Trace the angels on the opposite page and cut them out.
2. Punch a small hole at the top of each angel.
3. Look up all the references about angels you can find in the Bible. (The website www.biblegateway.com is a wonderful tool for doing this.)
4. Choose a favorite verse for each of the seven categories; use a marker to write one verse on each angel.
5. Use different lengths of yarn to attach each angel to a coat hanger. Space your angels apart so that your mobile hangs evenly.
6. Before you go to sleep, recite one or two of the verses. And then sleep well, knowing that God never sleeps and that His angels are at His command concerning you—to guard, protect, warn, inform, and keep you from fear and disaster. *Now isn't that a blessing?!*

He will command his angels concerning you to guard you in all your ways.

Psalm 91:11

87

When You Rise...

You probably wouldn't think of going outside without an umbrella during a rainstorm or without your coat, a hat, and boots when snow is falling. But sometimes we do something even crazier: We go out into the world—to school or to work—without getting ourselves ready to stand strong against both the attacks of Satan and the influences of the world around us (EPHESIANS 10:12).

We can get ready for those battles by filling our mind and feeding our soul with God's truth, by hiding His Word in our heart. And first thing in the morning, when our minds are rested and alert, is a very good time to work on memorizing Scripture. The Bible talks about putting on a soldier's equipment. Paul calls it the "armor of God" and lists its components: the breastplate of righteousness; the helmet of salvation; the shoes of preparation of the gospel of peace; the shield of faith; and the sword of the Spirit, which is the Word of God (see Ephesians 6:10–18).

So before anyone in your family goes out into the world today, make sure you're all protected by the Word of God. Here are some ways to do just that!

In the morning, O LORD, you hear my voice; in the morning I lay my requests before you and wait in expectation.

Psalm 5:3

Protection Against the Elements

Just as warm clothes protect us from the cold wind, rain, and snow of winter, God's armor protects us from the spiritual elements that would attack us. "We do not wrestle against flesh and blood, but against the rulers, against the authorities, against the cosmic powers over this present darkness, against the spiritual forces of evil in the heavenly places" (Ephesians 6:12, ESV). So remember to put on the "armor of God" before starting your day!

You'll find a description of the armor in Ephesians 6:14–18, "Stand therefore, having fastened on the belt of truth, and having put on the breastplate of righteousness, and, as shoes for your feet, having put on the readiness given by the gospel of peace. In all circumstances take up the shield of faith, with which you can extinguish all the flaming darts of the evil one; and take the helmet of salvation, and the sword of the Spirit, which is the word of God, praying at all times in the Spirit, with all prayer and supplication" (ESV).

To help you deliberately put on these pieces of armor, mark or sew labels on the different pieces of your winter clothing:

Coat—Button up that breastplate of righteousness!

Scarf—Wrap that belt of truth around you!

Hat—Make sure your helmet of salvation is on firmly!

Boots—Now you're shod with the preparation of the gospel!

Pray together before each person in your family leaves for work or school so that all of you are also fully equipped with:

- The shield of faith (Ephesians 6:16), which can extinguish all the flaming darts of the enemy.
- The sword of the spirit, which is the Word of God (Ephesians 6:17).
- Prayer (Ephesians 6:18).

To God be the glory as you serve Him throughout your day!

Blessings Throughout Your Day

When you read through the Bible, you'll see that children need their parents' blessing, soldiers going to battle need the blessing of their superiors and their countrymen, we believers need each other's blessing, and we all need God's blessing. Certain Scripture verses tell us that we can even "bless God" through our obedience and praise!

- Pray God's blessing on the day before you get out of bed.
- Bless your food and each other as you gather around the table to eat.
- Husbands, bless your wives by affirming them and assuring them of your love, your faithfulness, and your appreciation of all that they do.
- Wives, bless your husbands by telling them that you love them, respect them, and will be praying for them throughout the day.
- Parents, give your children your blessing before they leave for school. Tell them that you are proud of them and pray with them about their day. Tuck notes in their lunchboxes to remind them that you're praying for them. Ask God to use them as a witness to His love.
- Children, bless your parents by telling them that you love them, that you love God, and that you promise to represent your home with honor and integrity.
- Write a blessing and stick it on the dashboard of the car, mail it in a letter, or, if you won't be home at night, leave it on a family member's pillow.
- Look up the word *bless* (or *blessing*) in a good Bible concordance and spend family worship time reading together in God's Word about the blessings that people give and receive.

- Bless the "mission" or special assignment you've been given for the day. Here are some of the possibilities:
  * Going on a business trip on behalf of your boss.
  * Facilitating an important meeting.
  * Contacting someone who is hurting.
  * Coming alongside someone who is discouraged, who is ill, or who has a new baby.
  * Representing your class or team at a special school event.
  * Interviewing for a new job or a job promotion.
  * Gathering neighborhood friends for a Bible study.
  * Beginning a new grade, entering a new school, starting a new job, etc.

Death and life are in the power of the tongue.
Proverbs 18:21, ESV

The Surprise Blessing

The time had come. It was the first day of school. My precious first grader and I bravely drove the two blocks to the school.

As we pulled into the parking lot, I looked at Jenny. She had spent one year in the safe environment of a loving Christian kindergarten, but now it was time to enter public school—first grade. Apprehension was written across her face. How could I help her deal with this new situation? Nothing I said made her smile. Finally, I did what seemed to be silly, but it was what God was telling me to do. I blessed her. Placing my hand on her head, I prayed, "The LORD bless you and keep you; the LORD make his [smiling] face to shine upon you…and give you peace" (Numbers 6:24–26).

After she left, I stayed in the car, praying for the school, and thinking about blessing Jenny. I could not remember being blessed by my parents when I was a child. Where had this idea come from? I had never blessed my children before; I had never put my hand on their heads and pronounced God's blessing on them. Just doing it made me realize that the Bible is full of examples of people blessing their children. Joseph, Jacob, Isaac—to name a few—put great store in the words they prayed over a child's head. What a powerful tool God had put in my hands!

As the years went by and our fourth child, Crystal, went to school, blessing my children became a habit. Because Crystal's dad sometimes took her to school, she taught him to give her the blessing. If I forgot, she reminded me. This interaction with her was a daily joy to me.

The time with Jenny, however, became difficult. She was in junior high, the age when no one wanted to be different. She still wanted to be blessed, but her plea was "Mom, please don't let any of my friends see us!" I found it hard not to laugh since the prayer was very short and I said it in the car with the windows rolled up. "Okay, Jen, I'll make it short, and I won't put my hand on your head." So I put my hand on her shoulder, but in my heart it always rested on her head.

One day Jenny shyly came into my room and put a note on my desk. In it she thanked me for praying for her. Included in the note was a little card for my wallet imprinted with "our" blessing. It was her way of returning the blessing to me. A simple act on her part and a sweet message from God: *This is something I have established.* I know this God-given habit will continue into our adult lives together, and the words will sound even sweeter when they're "Grandma's blessing."

Kathy Maxwell, Monrovia, California

Not many of us would ever volunteer for pain and suffering. Yet, if we truly believe what the apostle Peter wrote, maybe more of us should!

In his first letter to some fellow believers, Peter explained that trials "come so that your faith—of greater worth than gold, which perishes even though refined by fire—may be proved genuine and may result in praise, glory and honor when Jesus Christ is revealed" (1 Peter 1:7).

Belief comes more easily when life is going well, when the road we're walking is straight and smooth. When unexpected pain comes, when the path we're walking gets rocky, we need fellow believers to come alongside us, to pray for us and to believe in us when we're struggling to do both.

Family members can offer each other that kind of support—and may each of you be blessed as you are a blessing to brothers and sisters, to Mom and Dad!

Respect those who work hard among you,
who are over you in the Lord and who admonish you.
Hold them in the highest regard in love because of their work.
Live in peace with each other.
And we urge you...encourage the timid,
help the weak, be patient with everyone.
Make sure that nobody pays back wrong for wrong,
but always try to be kind to each other....
1 Thessalonians 5:12–15

Casting Out Fear

Many times the unknown is at the root of our fears. Often, when we finally look directly at the thing we fear, it isn't so scary anymore. Especially when we remember, as we look at our fears, that Jesus is standing with us! It also helps to know that Someone who loves us, an infinitely powerful Someone, knows about our fears and is always there to calm us and to protect us.

- As you go around your family circle, take turns sharing some things that make you afraid. It may surprise the children to learn that parents also have fears. But be selective about what you share so that you don't unintentionally add to your children's fears!

- Pray about all the fears that were mentioned and commit those situations and each person to God's keeping.

- Promise to pray for each other. Assure your children that you are available to pray—even in the middle of the night—if they wake up afraid.

WORDS OF HOPE, WORDS OF PEACE

- Only Jesus can truly calm the storms of our lives, so look to Him. (Matthew 8:23–27)
- True love—that comes from God—gets rid of fear. (1 John 4:7–12)
- Sometimes life seems to be better or easier for people who aren't trying to follow Jesus and sometimes you can feel panicked about all the wrongdoing that's around you. (Psalm 55:16–23)
- Trust God to carry out justice and punish wrongdoers. (Deuteronomy 32:35; Romans 12:19)
- Encourage each other, especially when one of you is feeling weak. (Isaiah 35:3–4)

Check these verses out, too: Psalm 23:4; 27:1; Isaiah 51:7.

So do not fear, for I am with you;
do not be dismayed, for I am your God.
I will strengthen you and help you;
I will uphold you with my righteous right hand.

Isaiah 41:10

The Power of Fire

When we intentionally do things we know hurts others and makes God sad, we need powerful help to quit doing them. Hurting others, ourselves, and God is called "sin." The Bible says we need to confess (admit) these things (sins) and ask God and others to forgive us. Use a campfire, the family fireplace, or a chimenea to remind each other about the power of God's love to get rid of sin in our lives.

- Let each person in the family confess two or three things in their lives that make God sad.
- Collect a pile of sticks and have each family member give a stick the name of one of the sins.
- One by one, throw each stick into the fire. Ask your powerful and loving God to help you get rid of your sin just as the fire burns up and gets rid of the sticks.

If anyone does not remain in me,
he is like a branch that is
thrown away and withers;
such branches are picked up,
thrown into the fire and burned.

John 15:6

Being a Peacemaker

Who is the family neatnik—and who is the family…uh…slob? Who is the family pack rat—and who doesn't save anything? Which ones are the night owls—and which are the early risers? Which family member tends to procrastinate—and which one jumps into projects right away? Who is always patient—and who has a very short fuse?

With families made up of such different personalities and habits, occasional disagreements and conflicts are inevitable. Thankfully, God's Word tells us how to resolve conflict without hurting each other.

HERE ARE A FEW SUGGESTIONS FOR EVERYONE IN THE FAMILY:

- During several family worship times, discuss the "Thoughts to Consider" verses on the following page. Read the Scripture verses out loud and talk about what God is calling you to do. Remind each other that when God calls us to do something, He will give us the ability to obey!
- On a sheet of paper, write down the verses that seem especially important to your family. Post it where everyone will see it often (on the refrigerator, the kitchen bulletin board, etc.).
- Ask God to—by the power of His Spirit—keep your love for each other at the forefront of your minds, especially when conflict arises.
- Acknowledge that as long as sinners are living together under the same roof—and that's not a bad definition of "family"!—there will be conflicts and disagreements. Explain that, in light of that fact, family members need to be committed to resolving conflict. During a family worship time, promise each other that you will work through conflicts. The key to fulfilling that promise is choosing to value relationships over having your own way! Opt to be a peacemaker, not a peace breaker!

Thoughts to Consider

Constructive Conflict

- Seek peace, resolution, and reconciliation (Matthew 5:9).
- Speak words "seasoned with grace" (Colossians 4:6; Ephesians 4:29).
- Be quick to listen (James 1:19).

- Show healthy, appropriate anger and passion of commitment (Ephesians 4:26).
- Stay focused on the current issue.

- Talk about your feelings in response to the conflict. Be sure to use the personal pronoun "I" more than "you."
- Address the conflict with an attitude of humility, grace, mercy, and gentleness (Galatians 6:1–2).

- Know that some conflicts might take a long time to resolve. "Hang tough and tender" even if you have to love from afar for a season. Guard your heart and your tongue (Hebrews 12:14–15).

Destructive Conflict

- Use words to gain power even if you hurt someone in the process.
- Seek victory, vindication, and vengeance (Galatians 5:15).
- Be quick to speak, interrupt, attack, and defend yourself.
- Show destructive anger or hostility (Ecclesiastes 7:9).

- Rehearse a long history of related and unrelated incidents.
- Talk about the other person's faults and failures. Be sure to use the words "always" and "never."

- Address the conflict with an attitude of self-righteousness, a quest for power and words that blame and shame (2 Corinthians 12:20).
- If you don't win, bail out and move on. Someone, somewhere, will agree with you and like you. Grow bitter and and gossip as much as you can about the person with whom you disagreed.

When the Going Gets Tough

Bad things happen in life. Jesus Himself promised that we'd have trouble and tribulations in this world, so we shouldn't be surprised when we suffer and hurt (John 16:33). And when someone we know—someone in our family—is going through hard times, we need to be ready to come alongside and be God's light and love. Here are some tips.

- ❤ Be sensitive enough to notice when there is a problem. Learn to know each other so well that you can "read" each other even when words aren't spoken.
- ❤ Don't wait for the problem to pass. The situation may change and the pain may fade, but that family member may become resentful and bitter in the process.
- ❤ Encourage the person who is hurting to talk about the problem—and then listen with all your heart.
- ❤ Never belittle someone's feeling. Don't ever say, "Big boys/girls don't cry," or "It's silly to feel that way."
- ❤ When crisis strikes someone in your family, give that person top priority in terms of prayer, compassion, and support.
- ❤ When a crisis hits Mom and Dad, children can sense their deeper feelings. So, parents, discuss the situation honestly; don't lie. Confess your failure, lack of ability, or shortcomings to the degree that your children can handle it. Most important, let your children see that you turn to God for hope and peace, for forgiveness and love, for wisdom and direction.
- ❤ Forgive the person/people behind the hurt just as Jesus would.
- ❤ Consult the Bible for help understanding the situation and deciding what you should do.

- Pray together not so much that the problem will go away, but that God will bring comfort, growth, and wholeness to everyone involved. Pray in love for the hurtful person.
- Find creative ways as a family and as individuals to constructively channel energy that might otherwise have been wasted on hatred, resentment, and bitterness.
- Thank your sovereign God for the experience and for the way He will redeem it—and return good for the harm that was done to you.

Hang Your Prayers Up to Dry!

Write a prayer request on each cloud. Below it, write a promise from God that fits the situation.

- "Come to me, all you who are weary and burdened, and I will give you rest. Take my yoke upon you and learn from me, for I am gentle and humble in heart, and you will find rest for your souls. For my yoke is easy and my burden is light." – Matthew 11:28–30
- "I will always guide you and satisfy you with good things. I will keep you strong and well. You will be like a garden that has plenty of water that never runs dry." – Isaiah 58:11 (AMPLIFIED)
- "If any of you lacks wisdom, he should ask God, who gives generously to all without finding fault, and it will be given to him." – James 1:5
- "Cast all your anxiety on him because he cares for you." – 1 Peter 5:7

- "Look at the birds of the air; they do not sow or reap or store away in barns, and yet your heavenly Father feeds them. Are you not much more valuable than they? Who of you by worrying can add a single hour to his life?… So do not worry…your heavenly Father knows that you need [clothes and food]. But seek first his kingdom and his righteousness, and all these things will be given to you as well." – Matthew 6:26–27,31–33
- "He will not allow you to be tempted beyond what you can bear. But when you are tempted, he will also provide a way out so that you can stand up under it." – 1 Corinthians 10:13
- "Submit yourselves therefore to God. Resist the devil and he will flee from you. Draw near to God and he will draw near to you." – James 4:7–8 (ESV)
- "If we confess our sins, he is faithful and just and will forgive us our sins and purify us from all unrighteousness." – 1 John 1:9
- "Even though I walk through the valley of the shadow of death, I fear no evil, for You are with me; Your rod and Your staff, they comfort me." – Psalm 23:4 (NASB)
- "As a mother comforts her child, so will I comfort you." – Isaiah 66:13

When You Sit at the Table

The dinner table is one of the best places for great family time. Questions can be asked and answered. Warmhearted laughter can season the conversation. As family members share a meal, they also share about their day, and God can bless them with compassion, joy, and love as they do so.

The dinner table can also be a place where God reveals more of His truth and more of Himself. Below you'll find some ideas for making mealtimes more intentional times of being in God's presence and being nourished by His Word. Bon appétit!

"Man does not live on bread alone, but on every word that comes from the mouth of God."
Matthew 4:4

Holy Hors d'Oeuvres

Every night for a week have family members come to the dinner table ready to recite a verse about food or the table. Before thanking God for the food you're about to enjoy, give everyone an opportunity to recite the memorized verse.

   Here are some verses folks could learn:

   Vegetables: Numbers 11:5

   Table: Exodus 25:23; Psalm 23:5

   Raisins and Figs: 1 Samuel 25:18; 30:11–12

   Fish: Matthew 14:15–21; John 21:9

   Milk: Genesis 18:8; 1 Peter 2:1–3; Hebrews 5:12–14

   Bread: Exodus 13:6; 1 Samuel 17:17; Matthew 4:4; 2 Kings 4:42

   Honey: Genesis 43:11; Matthew 3:4

   Oil: Exodus 40:9; Leviticus 2:5; Psalm 23:5; Proverbs 21:20; James 5:14

   Cheese: Genesis 18:8; 1 Samuel 17:18; Isaiah 7:15, 22

   Locusts: Deuteronomy 28:38; Matthew 3:4

   Olives: Deuteronomy 7:13, NLT; Ezekiel 27:17, AMPLIFIED

   Pomegranates: Deuteronomy 8:8, THE MESSAGE

   Grapes: Numbers 13:23; Leviticus 19:10

   Meat: Exodus 12:8; Leviticus 8:31

   Barley: Ruth 2:23; 2 Samuel 17:28; 2 Kings 4:42

   Wheat: Deuteronomy 8:8, THE MESSAGE; Luke 6:1

   These verses from the Word of God may be the perfect appetizers for the dinnertime fellowship to come!

Meals à La Scripture

During His years walking this earth, Jesus often "broke bread" with His friends. Mary and Martha had Him as well as His disciples over for dinner (John 12:1–2). Toward the end of His life, He looked forward to celebrating the Passover with His disciples (Luke 22:15). And even the resurrected Christ enjoyed some cooked fish with his friends (Luke 24:41–43).

The Bible—Old Testament and New—contains many references to meals. Do some research in Bible dictionaries or on the Internet. Then use your imagination and try to recreate those meals. Serve the food mentioned and assign different family members the role of a person who was present at the meal. Have those family members either tell or act out the mealtime incident reported in Scripture. And while you're at it remember… *love* can be served up in ample portions around a dinner table. Jesus Himself knew that. Have fun!

A simple meal with love is better than a feast where there is hatred.
Proverbs 15:17, CEV

Here are a few ideas to get you started:
- The Last Supper – Mark 14:22; Luke 22:7–39
- The Feast of the Tabernacles – Leviticus 23:34–44
- On the road to Emmaus – Luke 24:13–35
- Elijah's two meals – 1 Kings 17:2–16
- Hillside picnic of bread and fish – John 6:9–13
- Feast for the prodigal son – Luke 15:11–24
- Fish barbecue on the beach – John 21:1–14
- Wedding feast in Cana, where Jesus performed His first miracle – John 2:1–11

Can you find references to other Bible meals? (You'll probably want to pass on John the Baptist's locusts and honey.) Enjoy the search—and the dining!

Who Turned Out the Lights?

Have you ever wondered what being blind would be like? Those of us with eyes that work cannot fully appreciate the miracle Jesus did when He healed a man who had been blind since birth (John 9:10–11). This man had never watched the changing colors of a sunrise or seen his mother smile at him. And when he sat down to dinner, someone had to tell him what kind of food was on the table.

EXTRA NAPKINS ALL AROUND!

1. Tonight, when you set the table for dinner, give everyone an extra napkin and a safety pin. Before you serve the meal, help everyone blindfold themselves with the napkin. Explain that you are going to have dinner without using your eyes and then give everyone a plate of food. Tell family members that instead of saying the usual "Thank You, God, for this food" prayer before eating the meal, you will wait until *after* dinner to pray. The prayers may be very different from your usual thanksgiving!

2. After dinner have people remove their blindfolds. Take turns reading the verses in John 9 that tell about Jesus' miracle.
    - Why was the man blind?
    - What did Jesus do to heal the man?
    - What did the man have to do in order to see?
    - Why did people doubt the miracle?

WHAT DO YOU THINK?

Does God do miracles today? What is a miracle? What miracles do you need Jesus to do for you? What do you need to do in order to receive His miracle? What are some everyday miracles that we are blind to?

Finally, close the mealtime with prayer. Give thanks to God for your sight and for His miracles, *especially* the miracles we have in our everyday lives. And pray for each other, asking God to meet the needs that were shared and to give everyone in the family eyes to see His work in their lives.

Let There Be Light— in Your Centerpiece

1. Write or type out each of the verses listed below on yellow five-by-seven-inch cards. For fun, cut each card into the shape of a star, moon, sun, or flame of fire.
   - How did we get light? (Genesis 1:3–5)
   - What if I'm afraid? Who is my light? (Psalm 27:1)
   - How should I live? (Ephesians 5:8)
   - What did Jesus say we are? (Matthew 5:14)
   - Who is the light of the world? (John 8:12)
   - Why is the Word of God important for each of us? (Psalm 119:105)
2. Ask each question and then read the passage that answers it. Talk about the verse and challenge family members to memorize it.
3. Put six bulky candles in a cluster on a plate and place it in the center of your table. Each time a verse is memorized by a family member, let that person light a candle for the evening meal. Automatically light the same candles the next night and the next, until all six are burning!

Your word is a lamp to my feet
and a light for my path.
Psalm 119:105

Building One Another Up

Have you ever thought—*really* thought—about the fact that your sister or mother or daughter is your sister in God's family? Or that your brother or father or son is your brother in the Lord? That fact can certainly transform how we view and how we treat members of our family!

God's Word tells us to build up the body of Christ—and that this practice can and should start at home. Here are some specific instructions:

- Be submissive to each other in love (take turns!) and always be submissive to God (obey His commands!). (Ephesians 5:21; James 4:7)
- Be willing to forgive—and quick to do so. (Matthew 6:14; Philippians 2:5)
- Share what you have and do so cheerfully. (Matthew 5:41; 2 Corinthians 8:3–5)
- Be eager to believe the best about a brother or sister in the Lord, and defend them when someone criticizes or attacks them with ugly words. (1 Corinthians 13:6–7)

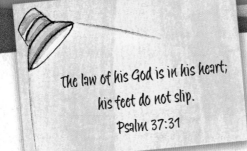

The law of his God is in his heart;
his feet do not slip.
Psalm 37:31

- Get together often and keep the lines of communication open. (Act 2:42)
- Be patient with each other. People don't mature overnight. (1 Thessalonians 5:14)
- When we love others the way we want to be loved, everyone wins. (Philippians 2:1–4)
- Encourage and affirm anyone who has failed at something or is feeling inadequate. (Hebrews 3:13)
- Talk together about the things that are bothering you, and pray for each other. (Galatians 6:2)

Yes, remembering that our family members are also members of the body of Christ could transform our relationships with each other. And by God's grace that transformation comes—powered by His Spirit and fueled by His Word, *hidden in your heart!*

Bibliography

Children's Bibles

NIRV Kids' Quest Study Bible (Zondervan, 1998) Created especially for beginning readers.

The Beginner's Bible (Zondervan, 1997) Ninety-five classic Bible stories with colorful cartoon illustrations.

NIRV Read with Me Bible (Zondervan, 2000) Bible story book with 106 stories for ages 4–8.

Egermeiers' Bible Story Book by Elsie E. Egermeier (Warner, 1969) Classic, reliable, excellent for ages 2+.

Hands-On Bible New Living Translation (Tyndale House, 2005) Fun and faith-building lessons for ages 6–10.

Kid's Life Application Bible New Living Translation (Tyndale Kids, 2000) "Heroes and Villains" profiles, "I Wonder" question notes, "Amazing Facts" Scripture references, and "Sticky Situations" decision-making stories for ages 8–12.

Middle School

Magnify: The Complete New Testament for Kids (Nelson, 2005) The International Children's Bible in a magazine format with articles, quizzes, and interactive games for ages 7 to 11.

NLT One-Year Bible for Kids Challenge Edition (Tyndale, 2004) Will help 8- to 12-year-olds read the bulk of God's Word in a year.

NIV Teen Study Bible (Zondervan, 2004) "Direct Line" life applications for ages 12–15.

NIV Teen Devotional Bible (Zondervan, 1999) Contains 260 devotionals written for teens by youth leaders and other teens.

Teen Girls

Revolve, The Complete New Testament for Girls (Nelson, 2003) Looks like a fashion magazine and includes on its glossy pages discussions of inner beauty and "Truth or Dare" challenges about values.

Revolve: Psalms, Proverbs, and Wisdom Literature (Nelson, 2004) "Guys Speak Out," "Beauty Secrets," and "Blab Q&A's" in a worship-themed, high-gloss issue.

NIV True Images (Zondervan, 2004) Includes "Love Notes from God" for young women ages 13–16.

Teen Boys

Refuel, The Complete New Testament for Boys NCV (Nelson, 2004) NCV with relevant points of application in an appealing, high-gloss format like a sports or entertainment magazine.

NIV Revolution: The Bible for Teen Guys (Zondervan, 2003) Strong male role models and father figures from Scripture, the invitation to question the messages of secular media, and the challenge to 13- to 16-year-olds to think before they act.

College

NRSV The Student Bible (Zondervan, 1996) Contains introductions to "100 People You Should Know" and other features from Philip Yancey and Tim Stafford.

NIV Student Bible (Zondervan, 2002) A year-long tour of the Bible led by Philip Yancey and Brenda Quinn.

NIV Study Bible (Zondervan, 2002) Features an outline and introduction to every book plus 20,000 in-text study notes.

Adult

Life Application Study Bible (Tyndale, 1997) Geared to helping you live what you learn.

The Thompson Chain-Reference Bible (NIV with Nelson Bibles, 2004; KJV with Kirkbride, 1993; NIV with Kirkbride, 2004)) Covering more than 7,000 topics, the verse chains in the margin follow a subject—person, place, idea—through the entire Bible.

Women's Devotional Bible (Zondervan, 1990) Devotionals written by more than one hundred well-known authors.

The Message: The Bible in Contemporary Language by Eugene Peterson (NavPress, 2002) Translated directly from Hebrew and Greek and designed to be read.

Games

Outburst: Bible Edition (TaliCor) Shout out answers to guess the ten target answers.

Bible Trivia Game (Cadaco) Trivia from the Old and the New Testaments, plus children's questions so all ages can play.

Scattergories: Bible Edition (TaliCor) List as many Bible items in the category mentioned and get a point for every answer you have that no one else does.

Acknowledgments

My thanks to my parents, who early on gave me a love for the Scriptures and daily lived out their truth in our home, and to my sister, Evelyn, who, because she shared the same heritage, believed in the value of this project and gave me encouragement all along the way.

To Simon Wesley Hayes who helps me recognize the eternal in every moment.

And to my own precious family, who is daily reinforcing my conviction that God's Word is a "lamp unto our feet and a light unto our path," even in the moral labyrinth of these new millennium days.

My gratitude, to my assistants, Teri Garner and Carma Wood, who share my passion for words and for the Word.

—Gloria

I'd like to express my gratitude to my mother, Alma Kubishta, who knew she needed divine assistance in raising her two children. She sent us to Sunday School and Christian camps where we learned the Scriptures and found an anchor for our lives. At a time when difficult circumstances were swirling around us, we were held steady by the eternal truths of God's Word. That is why I wanted to write this book with Gloria Gaither. Today's children, living in a time of moral freefall, need that same foundation in the Scriptures. As the Psalmist wrote, "The word have I hid in my heart, that I might not sin against thee" (Psalm 119:11, KJV).

I also want to thank my husband, who consistently lives out God's word in public and in private. Thank you, Jim, for your unwavering support, love and loyalty.

—Shirley